PHYSICIAN, HEAL THYSELF...

PHYSICIAN, HEAL THYSELF...

JOHN M. ALLEGRO

Prometheus Books
Buffalo, New York

Published 1985 by
Prometheus Books
700 E. Amherst Street, Buffalo, New York 14215

Copyright © 1985 by John M. Allegro

Printed in the United States of America

Library of Congress Catalogue Card No. 85-043081
ISBN 0-87975-305-6

Contents

Chapter One

Heavenly Secrets

Being born, and dying, mark the boundaries of our consciousness, and only the body's uncertain balance between health and sickness hold them apart. Small wonder that the mysteries of the healing arts have commanded so much of man's attention through the ages, or that they should have been attended by such fearful credulity.

This book is about the activities of a Jewish sect called Physicians, who believed that through powers granted to them by their God they could lead men from the shadow of death into new life, physical, mental, and spiritual. Their successors, called Christians, were charged with the same task; and through the centuries, despite the opposition of many within their own ranks, they have tried to discharge that sacred calling. Today their prophets and practitioners claim no less authority over mortal ills than did their spiritual forebears, through a conviction as firmly held of their right of direct access to the throne of Grace, and of their power to mediate that knowledge of God to their fellow men. It is not part of this study to confirm or cast doubt upon either the religious validity of these claims or their therapeutic efficacy, but merely to examine the origins and literary basis for the phenomenon of faith, or spiritual, healing within Christianity.

Other Aramaic-speaking Jews called the sectarians '*Asayya*', Healers, Physicians, or, in the Greek, *Essenoi*, *Essaioi*, Essenes; they called themselves the Sons of Light, the Elect, Men of the

(New) Covenant, Sons of God, Those of The Way, the Party (or Council) of the Community, and other titles denoting their special standing of pre-election and religious elitism. Much of what they believed of their calling and their mission we had known until recently only from hearsay, through the writings of such ancient historians as Philo Judaeus, Pliny the Elder, and above all, Josephus, writing in the first century. We knew that they were an exclusive sect, with their headquarters near the northern end of the Dead Sea, but with lay communities scattered near towns and villages all over Palestine. Josephus ranks them with the Pharisees and the Sadducees, but makes it clear that they were not an open order. They required of those who sought to join their community a period of strict probation during which they would have to demonstrate their sincerity and conviction of their vocation. They were expected to live an ascetic existence, on a sparse and highly regulated diet, and for most of them without the company of women. Their social and personal discipline evoked much wonder and admiration among their fellow men, but it is clear that those outside the order were not allowed to know their most cherished doctrines, which were passed on among themselves orally and under the strictest vows of secrecy.

They believed that God had called them to maintain the true faith of Israel until His Messiah, or Christ, should come to institute the Heavenly Kingdom on earth and the beginning of the Millennium, the thousand years of unchallenged theocracy when all nature would be changed and the Golden Age inaugurated. Until then, the Essenes had cut themselves off from the rest of Judaism because it seemed to them that their co-religionists in the cities had compromised with their political masters and betrayed their traditional teachings, revealed by God to Moses and interpreted thereafter by the prophets and their own leader, the so-called Teacher of Righteousness.

As well as the whole body of the Jewish Law, or Torah, the Physicians seem to have imbibed many occult teachings, including astrology and a dualistic view of the universe, which were not of the Jewish tradition but sprang from the kind of Persian philosophy embedded in Zoroastrianism. Some of their sages were reputed to be clairvoyants, "and seldom, if ever," says Josephus, "do they err in their predictions" (*War* II, 159). They were also famed as physicians, as their name indicates, and he says of them:

> They display an extraordinary interest in the writings of the ancients, singling out in particular those which make for the welfare of soul and body; with the help of these, and with a view to the treatment of diseases, they make investigations into medicinal roots and the properties of minerals [lit: "stones"]. [*War* II, 136]

But despite the claims of Josephus to have been once a full-fledged member of the Order of Essenes, in fact it was not until 1947, when a chance find in a cave near the northwestern shores of the Dead Sea produced some ancient scrolls from their library, that we were able to read first-hand accounts of what they believed and how they saw their place in the divine plan. And even now, forty years on, we can claim to have lifted the veil only the proverbial inch or two. At the time of this writing, much of what was recovered from the caves in the years subsequent to the initial discovery is not yet published, but even so it is clear that the innermost counsels of this hitherto shadowy group of Physicians will remain forever shrouded in mystery. So however privileged we are by being able after two millennia to read their writings, and even wander around the ruins of their Dead Sea settlement, we cannot expect ever to discover the occult formulae and practices that gave them their high reputation and their power.

The Physicians seem to have traced the origin of their access to divine wisdom to the age-old tradition of the fall of the angels. There is a brief reference to this portentous event in the book of Genesis (6:1-2):

> When men began to multiply on the face of the ground, and daughters were born to them, the sons of God saw that the daughters of men were fair; and they took to wife such of them as they chose . . . .

Of that unnatural union was born, as might have been expected, a race of supermen, or giants, called variously Nephilim ("Fallen Ones") or Rephaim, originally of similar meaning, but understood in a Semitic milieu at least as "Healers" (of the root *rph'*, "heal"). It was the corruption of their special knowledge then introduced into the world that brought mankind to the state of degradation when God had no option but to sweep away all life in the Flood and start again with Noah and those creatures he had brought with him in the Ark.

Although the Bible offers only a sparse note on the story of the fallen angels, the books of the pseudepigrapha, which the Essenes knew and copied copiously in their library, preserves current tradition in far more detail. From the book of Enoch we learn that among the divine secrets then revealed were the arts of enchantments, feminine cosmetics, and, above all, "the cutting of roots and acquaintance with plants" (7:1 ff.), that is, herbalism, the stock-in-trade of the traditional wise-man, witch-doctor, and physician down through the ages.

It was fitting then, that the Essenes should make the Dead Sea area their temporary home, for it was just there that the fallen angels lay imprisoned, as we learn from the visions of the patriarch Enoch. He tells us that the archangel Raphael ("God heals") was told to

bind Azazel [chief of the rebellious angels] hand and foot
and cast him into the darkness, and make an opening in the
desert . . . and place upon him rough and jagged rocks, and
cover his face that he may not see the light. And on the great
day of judgement he shall be cast into the fire. And heal the
earth which the angels have corrupted and proclaim the
healing of the earth, that they may heal the plague, and that
all the children of men may not perish through all the secret
things that the Watchers [the fallen angels] have disclosed
and have taught their sons. For the whole earth has been
corrupted through the works that were taught by Azazel: to
him ascribe all sin. [10:4-6]

Along with their chief most of the other angelic rebels
were locked in this abyss of judgement in the Palestinian Rift
Valley and left to languish there until the heavenly tribunal,
when they, along with all mankind, would be arraigned before
the Mercy Seat.

A more specific reference to this awesome location is made
later in the visions of Enoch:

And I saw that valley in which there was a great convulsion
and an upsurge of the waters. And when all this took place,
from that fiery molten metal and from the accompanying
upheaval there was produced a sulphurous smell associated
with those waters, and that valley of the angels who had led
mankind astray burned beneath that land. And through its
valleys proceed streams of fire, where these angels are punished who had led astray those who dwell upon the earth.
[67:5-7]

One could almost believe that the writer of this pseudepi-
graphical work was acquainted with the vast earth movements
that geologists tell us took place millions of years ago, when
the collapse of part of the earth's surface between two parallel

series of faults resulted in the formation of the great Rift Valley. But at least he was familiar with one piece of evidence of more recent volcanic activity in that area—the hot springs on the east side of the Jordan and the Dead Sea, such as were found by one Anah in the land of Edom, according to the genealogies of Esau's sons in the Book of Genesis (36:24). The Essenes were well aware that a more recent son of Edom, the ruthless King Herod, had recourse to the baths across the Dead Sea, at Callirrhoe, opposite their monastery, to cure him of his richly earned bodily ailments. For the court physicians also knew of the supposed demonic associations and therapeutic efficacy of the hot springs that bubbled out of the ground there, as Josephus records:

> From that time onwards Herod's malady began to spread to his whole body and his suffering took a variety of forms. He had fever, though not a raging fever, an intolerable itching of the whole skin, continuous pains in the intestines, tumours in the feet as in dropsy, inflammation of the abdomen and gangrene of the genitals, engendering worms, in addition to asthma, with great difficulty in breathing, and convulsions in all his limbs. His condition led diviners to pronounce his maladies a judgement on him for his treatment of the sophists. Yet, struggling as he was with such numerous complaints, he clung to life, hoped for recovery, and devised one remedy after another. Thus he crossed the Jordan to take the warm baths at Callirrhoe, the waters of which descend into the Lake Asphaltitis [the Dead Sea, so named from the lumps of bitumen that were said to float upon its waters] and are drunk for their sweetness. [*War* I, 656-57]

So the writer of the Book of Enoch, continuing the seer's vision, identified the therapeutic baths by the Dead Sea with the fallen angels' underground prison:

But those waters shall in those days serve for the kings and the mighty and the exalted, and those who dwell upon the earth, for the healing of the body, but for the punishment of the spirit; now their spirit is full of lust, that they may be punished in their body, for they have denied the Lord of Spirits and see their punishment daily, and yet believe not in His name. And in proportion as the burning of their bodies becomes severe, a corresponding change shall take place in their spirit for ever and ever; for before the Lord of Spirits none shall utter an idle word . . . . [67:8-9]

Apparently it was believed that when the punishment of the rebellious angels had been completed, the waters of the hot springs would become cold and lose their healing efficacy; nevertheless the fires below ground would go on burning and what had once cured men's ills would then serve to punish their sins for eternity:

And those same waters will undergo a change in those days; for when the angels' punishment is complete in these waters, the springs will change their temperature. And when the angels ascend, the waters of the springs will change and become cold. . . . Because these waters of judgement minister to the healing of the angels' bodies and their lusts, they will not understand or believe that those same waters will become a fire which burns for ever. [67:10-13]

As late as the last century, popular belief held that the hot water of the springs was released from the lower regions by evil spirits merely to stop it being available to assuage the pains of the damned in hell. Another legend has it that King Solomon sent a servant to open the springs when he discovered how thin was the crust of the earth at this point. However, lest the threats of the subterranean demons should deter his messenger, the king had his eardrums pierced so that the man should not hear the continual wailing of the afflicted.

The angelic rebels then, steeped in heavenly knowledge, were reckoned to be imprisoned below ground at the very spot where the earth's crust was at its thinnest, and where men could at once benefit from its subterranean fires and at the same time be reminded of the awful fate that awaited the damned.

The idea that a reservoir of secret knowledge was stored beneath the ground goes back into the mists of time. In terms of fertility mythology, it has to do with the conception of the fructifying Word of God, the rain or dew, envisaged as divine semen impregnating the furrows of Mother Earth and so fathering the crops that gave food for man and beast. A great "sea of knowledge," as the ancients called it, was thus accumulated underground and could be tapped through the medium of especially powerful plants, better endowed than most with this wonderful seed of heaven. Herein lies the philosophy of herbal remedies, and also of those plants whose juices had the power to kill, or to offer the partaker a means of transporting his soul back to the source of Divine Knowledge in a hallucinatory trance (see the present writer's *Sacred Mushroom and the Cross*, 1970, p. 21).

A particularly potent form of this semen was the dew that the day-star Venus formed on the surface of the ground before the sun rose to burn it away with its heat. As Pliny says:

> Its influence is the cause of the birth of all things upon the earth; at both of its risings it scatters a genital dew with which it not only fills the conceptive organs of the earth, but also stimulates those of all animals . . . .

The dew could also be applied direct:

After the rising of each star, but particularly the principal stars, if rain does not follow but the dew is warmed by the rays of the sun . . . drugs (*medicamenta*) are produced, heavenly gifts for the eyes, ulcers, and internal organs. And if this substance is kept when the dog-star is rising, and if, as often happens, the rise of Venus or Jupiter or Mercury falls on the same day, its sweetness and potency for recalling mortals' ills from death is equal to the Nectar of the gods. [*Natural History*, II, 37, 38]

The prophet Isaiah echoed the same tradition when he looked for the manifestation of the spirits of the dead:

Thy dead shall live, their bodies shall arise.
   O dwellers in the dust, awake and sing for joy!
For thy dew is a dew of light,
   and on the land of the Shades [Rephaim] thou wilt
let it fall.

(26:19)

This same concept of the store of underground knowledge finds a further expression in the idea of necromancy, divination through the spirits of the dead. Isaiah speaks scornfully of such necromancers or ventriloquists ("belly-speakers") as "chirping and muttering" when they seek by oracle their god through "the dead, on behalf of the living" (8:19). However, King Saul was not averse to seeking advice from the dead prophet Samuel by such arts through the medium of the witch of Endor, despite the fact that in an earlier burst of pious enthusiasm the king had banished spiritualist mediums of her kind.

Then the woman said, "Whom shall I bring up for you?" He said, "Bring up Samuel for me." When the woman saw Samuel, she cried out with a loud voice; and the woman said

to Saul, "Why have you deceived me? You are Saul." The
king said to her, "Have no fear; what do you see?" And the
woman said to Saul, "I see a god coming up out of the
earth." He said to her, "What is his appearance?" And she
said, "An old man is coming up; and he is wrapped in a
robe." And Saul knew that it was Samuel . . . . [I Sam.
28:11-14]

Whether the Essenes in their monastic home sited over the
living tomb of the Rephaim practiced necromancy, we shall
probably never know. But it is not improbable that in their
small plantations nearby they grew the herbs they needed for
their healing practices and perhaps even those more powerful
drugs that would have released their souls for their perilous
journeys through the seven heavens to the Source of Knowledge. Certainly their traditions told them that God had granted
to some specially privileged mortals the antidotes to the
mischief wrought on mankind by the fallen angels. Another
apocryphal work, Jubilees, also favorite reading of the Essenes,
recalls that God allowed Noah to know

> all the medicines of their diseases, together with their seduc-
> tions, how he might heal them with herbs of the earth. And
> Noah wrote down all the things in a book as we instructed
> him concerning every kind of medicine. Thus the evil spirits
> were precluded from hurting the sons of Noah. And he gave
> all he had written to Shem, his eldest son, for he loved him
> exceedingly above all his sons. [10:12-15]

Those precious secrets were subsequently passed on to Jacob
from Abraham in his blessing (Jubilees 19:27-28), and from
Jacob to Levi "that he might preserve them and renew them
for his children" (45:16). They thus entered the protective
custody of the Levitical priesthood of the Jews, to whose order

the Essenes insisted their Guardians, or "bishops," should belong.

Long before the Dead Sea Scrolls were found, it had been suggested that the Essenes of Jewish history might turn out to be the "missing link" between normative Judaism and Christianity. This latter faith, ostensibly another Jewish sect, at least in its origins, has many puzzling features for the historian. Its founder was supposed to have been a Jewish teacher and his first followers compatriots sharing his ethnic and cultural background. Yet his relaxed attitudes toward the hated Roman authorities, his seemingly nonpolitical interpretation of the messianic ideal, his extension of the Jewish hopes to the Gentile world at large, as well as other anachronistic, linguistic, topographical, cultural, and religious inconsistencies in the Gospels, present problems to the critical observer that have never been resolved. Furthermore, the earliest writings in the New Testament, the letters of Saint Paul, expound a highly developed theology that is in many respects far removed from its Jewish fount, and sometimes seems to have more in common with the Greek mystery cults than the Semitic monotheism of the Old Testament and the rabbis. Whatever religious milieu gave birth to such a faith there seems little doubt that it was well outside the pale of normative first-century Palestinian Judaism.

Enough was known of Essenism to realize that it differed in many respects from contemporary Jewish orthodoxy, and that in its baptism of initiates, its ritual common meal, its ordering and internal discipline, its communism, its antagonism toward the Jewish hierarchy, and so on, there seemed a strong possibility that this sect might prove to be at least one of the stages that separate rabbinic Judaism from Christianity. The Dead Sea Scrolls have shown this to be the case. There are still very many differences, which the Christian apologists have not been slow to point out, and yet this larger picture of the faith of the Physicians that we have now before us shows enough in common with New Testament Christianity to lead to the conclusion that, whatever further developments took place in the formulation of its theology, the line of descent runs back through Essenism.

Among the many points of direct contact are the details of the internal ordering of the Essene community and the early Church, and particularly the office and functions of the Guardian mentioned above. It was early on pointed out by scholars that these were remarkably reminiscent of the Christian Bishop, whose Greek title, indeed, almost exactly reproduces the meaning of the Hebrew. As we shall see, his duties as laid down in the Essene manuals are just those attributed to the apostle Peter in the New Testament, including the exercise of his healing faculties, the secrets of which the Essenes believed had been transmitted to their Guardians through the fallen angels and the patriarchs. In these terms it could be claimed that the theory and practice of healing that runs throughout the history of the Church originated from the source of all wisdom, heaven itself.

Chapter Two

The Eye of Discernment

The stories of Jesus in the Gospels leave unclear his attitude toward the administration of the community he founded; he seems at times vague even about his precise mission. Direct questions on whether he was, or was not, the expected Messiah, or Anointed One—a vital matter to his followers—he parried, as though he wished the answer to be born of some inner conviction, either through divine revelation or from the effect of his personality on those with whom he came into contact. In the Gospel of Matthew it is Peter who first feels able to declare unequivocally that the Nazarene Teacher was indeed "the Christ, the son of the living God":

> Now when Jesus came into the district of Caesarea Philippi, he asked his disciples, "Who do men say that the Son of Man is?" And they said, "Some say John the Baptist, others say Elijah, and others Jeremiah or one of the prophets." He said to them, "But who do you say that I am?" Simon Peter replied, "You are the Christ, the Son of the living God." And Jesus answered him, "Blessed are you, Simon Bar-Jona! For flesh and blood has not revealed this to you, but my Father who is in heaven. And I tell you, you are Peter, and on this rock I will build my church, and the gates of hell shall not prevail against it. I will give you the keys of the kingdom of heaven, and whatever you bind on earth shall be bound in heaven, and whatever you loose on earth shall be loosed in heaven." [16:13-19]

So in the story, the revelation of Jesus' mission came to Peter not from hearsay or from common observation, but directly from Heaven, thus warranting the assumption that he stood in some special relationship with God. So Jesus could declare him a *Cephas* (John 1:42). The true significance of that name we can now recognize for the first time, thanks to the Dead Sea Scrolls.

A recently published scrap of parchment from the Qumran caves (see the appendix to the present writer's *The Dead Sea Scrolls and the Christian Myth*) gives what appears to be a transliterated form of this title as the author (or recipient) of a clinical report of treatment prescribed for sick visitors:

> The report of [to] the Caiaphas, being an account of his rounds of the afflicted [among] the guests: supplies of medicines [. . .]
>
> [. . .] swelling [. . .] which distended him through a kind of flabbiness due to wasting:—a braying of stalks of "Mephi-bosheth" in the . . .
>
> Hyrcanus Yannai's ulcer and its discharging secretions were drawn; also for Peter Yosai;
>
> Colic—Zachariel Yannai;
>
> Eli is witness, dictated by Omriel . . . .

The parchment surface is coarse and badly rubbed, the language an extraordinary mixture of transliterated Greek, Aramaic, and a grammatically irregular Hebrew, which gives the impression of deliberate obscurantism, not entirely unfamiliar in medical prescriptions even today, and perhaps even more applicable in a society so dedicated to secrecy. The official of the community who wrote this report (or to whom it was addressed) was apparently concerned with the day-to-day practice of healing, and the mention of "guests," or "strangers," would indicate that the monastery opened its doors to members from elsewhere who came to its clinic for treatment. (This could, incidentally, explain why a separate cemetery outside the walls contained the skeletons of women and children, otherwise difficult to explain in what one presumes to have been a celibate community.) A close examination of his title in this light reveals that what has hitherto been taken for no more than a "nickname" pressed by Jesus on Peter, based on a piece of linguistic word-play on his name Peter (*Petros*), the Greek word for "rock" (*petra*), and an Aramaic word *kepha'*, "stone," was in fact something of far more significance. In the Qumran text it is written in a way that suggests that Cephas may be only a variant form of the name Caiaphas, given to the High Priest's special functionary whose task it was to investigate the credentials of pretenders to the office of Messiah, or Christ. It will be recalled that it was this Caiaphas (some texts of the New Testament give the variant form *Caiphas*) who was a prominent member of the supreme council of the Jews, the Sanhedrin, at the time of Jesus' arraignment for heresy (John 18:13 f., 24, 28; Matt. 26:3, 57; etc.) and was responsible for conducting the investigation.

An examination of the history of the word in the Semitic languages makes its meaning plain. In ancient Akkadian the verbal root was used to mean "to scrutinize someone" with a view to entrusting that person with an appointment, and thus to ensure that he was "genuine, trustworthy." In line with this Arabic has the verb in the sense of "follow; examine, investigate," whence is derived "prognosticator, physiognomist." In Hebrew and Aramaic it came to have a very special, religious use.

The long-expected Messiah was to be identified by a number of important characteristics prophesied of him in the Bible, including his tribal origins (of the house of David), his place of birth (David's city, Bethlehem), the astrological portents that heralded his birth (the appearance of the "star out of

Jacob"—Num. 24:17), and even, as we now know from the Essene scrolls, his physical features. But to all these literary criteria, long rehearsed by the Jewish doctors of law, would have been the expectation that the Christ or Messiah should possess a special charisma recognizable only by those granted the discerning eye of the true Cephas/Caiaphas, prognosticator and visionary. John the Baptist is portrayed as having this discerning eye when, by the Jordan River, "he looked at Jesus" and recognized his unique relationship with God (John 1:36). Jesus believed that Peter, the humble fisherman, who had recognized the high calling of his Master where even the most learned rabbis of the Temple had been blinded by their preconceptions, had been so blessed, and thus merited the title. Similarly, Peter's other special designation, *Baryona*, misread (intentionally or otherwise) as if it were a patronymic, "Son of Jonah," is derived from an ancient Semitic root meaning "divine, foresee," whose origins connect it with a word for "physician."

So the power of foreknowledge, medical prognostication, and spiritual cognizance were regarded simply as related aspects of the one divine gift granted the Cephas/Caiaphas. In the healing stories of the New Testament there is a recurring emphasis upon the need for the physician to "look upon" the suppliant, as when the epileptic's father asked Jesus to "look upon my son" (Luke 9:38), and the Master was able to recognize and command the possessing demon to leave the lad in peace. Peter similarly "directed his gaze" at the congenitally lame man at the Temple gate, and invited him to concentrate all his attention upon himself in return. Then he was able to raise him to his feet (Acts 3:4-7). A parallel account of Saint Paul's healing activities has the apostle "looking intently" at a cripple and recognizing in him the power of faith that might give him strength to overcome a lifetime's disability (Acts 14:8-10). Small wonder that the biblical accounts of Peter's activities as Cephas and leading apostle among the Twelve, and later as head of the newly formed community of believers, should give pride of place to his powers of spiritual discernment and its pastoral accompaniment of healing.

For it is now clear that these New Testament stories, whatever their historicity, are in part anecdotal representations of the functions required of the community's chief administrator, or Bishop, and mirror exactly the requirements laid down in the Dead Sea Scrolls for the Essene Guardian, or Overseer. Josephus had earlier told us that the Essenes "elect officers to attend to the interests of the community, the special services of each officer being determined by the whole body" (*War* II, 123). It would appear that each establishment had one overall Overseer, the community "Bishop," but that in the regulative monastic center by the Dead Sea there were a number of departmental heads, including one specifically assigned to the clinic as Caiaphas. Peter is portrayed as undertaking the more general functions of the Essene Guardian, as well as the specialized role of a Caiaphas/Cephas, examiner and physician. When Jesus appoints him to be a "binder and looser" of men's sins (Matt. 16:19), Peter assumes the duties of the Guardian who "shall loosen all the fetters which bind them, that there be none in his congregation oppressed and broken," as one scroll puts it (Damascus Document, Col. XIII). In the stories of Peter's escapes from prison this metaphorical allusion to the fetters of sin is given a more literal presentation: "and the chains fell off his hands" (Acts 12:7; cf. 5:19). After Jesus' removal from the earthly scene, Peter takes up the role of "shepherd" to the community, as the Master had instructed him (John 21:15, 16). He is its administrator. He organizes the election by lots of a successor to the offending Judas (Acts 1:26), acts as bursar of the common purse (Acts 5:3), as earlier he had spoken for the company before the Temple tax officials (Matt. 17:24-27). He is the community's spokesman, a multilinguist, an instructor on the significance of recent history and the "mighty works and wonders" of God performed through Jesus (Acts 2:22). Even the hitherto obscure reference to his old age when he would stretch out his hands, "and another will gird you and carry you where you do not wish to go" (John 21:18) has now been set in its proper light. The appended "explanation" in the Gospel that it was an indication of the manner of the apostle's death is hardly justified by what appears to be no more than a casual observation on the helplessness of old age. In fact, the real significance of the passage is apparent from the regulation in one of the Essene documents that the Guardian "shall be from thirty to fifty years of age" (Damascus Document, Col. XIV). The reason for the comparatively early retirement of this important official is that he needed to be at the very peak of his intellectual abilities. He must be able to command the respect of his flock and not be swayed in matters of order and discipline by his inability to fend for himself.

Strict discipline in such a monastic community as the Essenes had founded by the Dead Sea was of the utmost importance. The so-called Manual of Discipline, which is one of the most important of the Scrolls recovered from the caves, reveals just how organized the lives of these "monks" were in all respects. In such extreme climatic and restricted conditions as their desert sojourn presented, it was necessary to demonstrate their "love for their neighbors" to a degree of tolerance beyond anything that might have been expected in more normal circumstances; they must not interrupt another brother when he was speaking in council, must control the urge to personal reproof, and if one member felt obliged to report a defaulting colleague to a higher authority, he must do it in a strictly regulated way, supported by a stipulated number of witnesses. The same rules are laid down for the community of

Christian believers and put into the mouth of Jesus (Matt. 18:15-17).

In matters requiring the examination of plaintiffs and witnesses, the discerning eye of the Caiaphas/Cephas would have played its part. So, in the story of Peter and the recalcitrant Ananias and Sapphira, who falsely declared the value of some real estate they had sold for donation to the common fund (again, a reflection of a similar regulation of the Essene covenanters), he was able to detect Ananias's guilt as soon as he appeared at the table, and not only thus brought about the man's death through a heart-attack, but prophesied that his wife in her complicity should follow him swiftly to the grave (Acts 5:1-10).

Healing was a spiritual exercise. All sickness was attributed to demonic possession and the essential prerequisite of any effective therapy was the identification and naming aloud of the evil spirit. "What is your name?" asked Jesus of the demon controlling the demented outcast of the Gerasene cemetery. He replied that his name was Legion, and, recognizing the superior power of the exorcist before him, begged that he be given the body of some other mortal creature to possess rather than be left to roam the world homeless for all eternity (Mark 5:1-20). To know the name of anyone was to have power over that person, for, in ancient lore, the name was not just a tag of identity; once given it became an essential part of its owner's corporate being. For a stranger to know someone's name was to gain a measure of control over him, much as medieval witches were thought to be able to wreak good or ill on anyone whose nail clippings or locks of hair they were able to acquire. On another plane, to know the name of the guardian angels was believed to guarantee their assistance in enabling the freed souls of Jewish mystics to penetrate the seven spheres of heaven, glimpse the heavenly throne, and return safely to their bodies. The Essenes believed they knew the names of these heavenly guardians, and had to swear that they would never divulge that knowledge to anyone outside the Order (Josephus, *War* II, 142). Even more essential was to know the name of God Himself, because only then was it possible for the humble believer to contact Him in prayer and make his request heard. Thus the revelation given to Moses on Mount Horeb of the deity's secret name (whose true pronunciation is still a matter for speculation) was regarded as a pivotal point in the story of Israel's attainment of nationhood; thenceforth her priests could call upon their tribal god to give his people supremacy over their mortal enemies. The name of the risen Jesus was similarly thought to accomplish miracles, since to know and pronounce it was to share in the Master's own power. Peter acknowledged to an investigatory council of the Sanhedrin that the healing of the cripple in Jerusalem had been accomplished "by the name of Jesus Christ of Nazareth" (Acts 4:10, 30).

Furthermore, a Cephas/Caiaphas could prognosticate the course of history as well as the progress of a patient's disease. "You know nothing at all," said Caiaphas to the other members of the Sanhedrin. "You do not understand that it is expedient for you that one man should die for the people, and that the whole nation should not perish." Thus, comments the writer of the Fourth Gospel, "he prophesied that Jesus should die for the nation" (John 11:49-51). Clairvoyance was similarly expected of the spiritually endowed, as the story of the onlookers' mockery of the condemned Jesus makes clear: "They also blindfolded him and asked him, 'Prophesy! Who is it that struck you?'" (Luke 22:64).

Josephus notes this of the Essenes:

There are some among them who profess to foretell the future, being versed from their early years in holy books, various forms of purification and sayings of prophets; and seldom, if ever, do they err in their predictions. [War II, 159]

The Dead Sea Scrolls refer to this special kind of enlightenment as "the Knowledge of God." It was a gift of grace, not bestowed on all men, but very precious since it gave access to the divine source of all wisdom. Greek writers called it *gnosis*, and those who claimed to have it, Gnostics. We know them best from Church history as the arch-heretics who created such divisory problems for the so-called Great Church in the first centuries. They believed that their special relationship with God was not dependent upon intermediaries, priestly or ecclesiastical, but was direct and personal. We shall see later how this individualism in Christianity, despite all its early persecution by the "orthodox" establishment, survived and flourished and became the Church's continuing witness to the healing tradition. For now, thanks to the Dead Sea Scrolls, we are able to appreciate as never before that spiritual healing in Christianity, as in its Jewish forerunner Essenism, was not a mere secondary aspect of the Church's work and witness: Historically it was central to its faith and practice. And in that title *Caiaphas/Cephas*, "spiritual discerner, physiognomist, prognosticator," lies the clue to the special gifts claimed by the Christian healer throughout history.

Chapter Three

The Knowledge of God

"Knowing God," in the mystical Essene/Christian sense, involved far more than the intellect: it was an illumination of the spirit, a revelation of divine mysteries, a participation in the godhead itself. For the Jew generally, the essence of all truth was and is the *Torah*, the Law, revealed to Moses and repeated after the entry in the Promised Land by his lieutenant Joshua, son of Nun. Among the Essenes, too, the Torah was the prime means of knowing God's will for man, and a prerequisite for salvation, but it had to be supplemented by the interpretation given by their own Lawgiver, the so-called Teacher of Righteousness. This whole body of revelation was divinely inspired and the ability to receive and adopt its instruction was no less God-given and a mark of divine election. Not every person could enter this state of grace: Only those chosen by God even before their conception could receive the light of inner perception. A hymn at the conclusion of the Essenes' Community Rule expresses this idea of justification and the imparting of the saving Knowledge of God to the believer:

> From the well of His righteousness
>   flows my justification,
> and from His marvellous mysteries
>   is the light of my heart.
> Mine eyes have gazed
>   on that which is eternal,

> on wisdom concealed from men,
>   on knowledge and cunning device
>   [hidden] from the sons of men;
> on a well of righteousness
>   and on a reservoir of strength,
> on a spring of glory
>   [hidden] from mortal counsel.
> To those whom He hath chosen
>   God has given these things
>   as an eternal possession,
> and has cast their inheritance
>   in the lot of the holy angels.
> He has joined their counsel
>   with the Sons of Heaven
> to be a Council of the Community,
>   that their conclave dwell
>   in the Abode of Holiness,
> an eternal Planting for all times.

The Teacher, to whose hand we might reasonably ascribe this and other hymns in the Essene library, speaks often of his insight into the wonderful mysteries, and there can be no doubt that he and those of his community who had attained to the inner circle of the elect believed themselves specially endowed with the ability to penetrate to the fount of all wisdom, God himself.

Jesus, also, acts as a Mediator of Knowledge to his followers:

> I thank thee, Father, Lord of heaven and earth, that Thou hast hidden these things from the wise and understanding, and revealed them to babes. . . . All things have been delivered to me by my Father; and no one knows the Son except the Father; and no one knows the Father except the Son, and anyone to whom the Son chooses to reveal Him. [Matt. 11:25-27]

Similarly, Saint Paul considered himself the instrument of God's revelation into the divine mysteries, "kept in silence through times eternal but now manifested" (Rom. 16:25-26), and writes in his first letter to the Corinthians:

> but we impart a secret and hidden wisdom of God, which God decreed before the ages for our glorification. . . . God has revealed to us through the Spirit. For the Spirit searches everything, even the depths of God. For what person knows a man's thoughts except the spirit of the man which is in him? So also no one comprehends the thoughts of God except the Spirit of God. Now we have received not the spirit of the world, but the spirit which is from God, that we might understand the gifts bestowed on us by God. And we impart this in words not taught by human wisdom but taught by the Spirit, interpreting spiritual truths to those who possess the Spirit. The unspiritual man does not receive the gifts of the Spirit of God, for they are folly to him, and he is not able to understand them because they are spiritually discerned. [2:7-14]

The believer can only receive the Knowledge of God through his predetermined suitability for the revelation, and by being shown the way by one who himself stands in a special relationship with God. Such a mediator will have the discerning eye of the Cephas/Caiaphas to estimate the spiritual aptitude of the initiate, and part of his judgement would derive from his knowledge of the supplicant's horoscope.

One of the scrolls from the Qumran library is an astrological work, written in code, and dealing with the influence of the stars on the physical and spiritual characteristics of persons born in certain sections of the zodiac. For example, a man born under Taurus, the Bull, could be expected to have long and lean thighs, narrow toes, and a humble demeanor. More important, he would have inherited a credit balance of good spirit against bad, in the proportion of six to three. On the other hand, a less favored person, cursed with a proportion of eight parts from the Pit of Darkness, as it was called, to only one from the House of Light, might be expected to display a somewhat coarse appearance, with broad, hairy thighs and short, stubby toes. The general rule seems to have been that the better endowed a person was spiritually, the more ascetic his appearance. Thus in direct opposition to the last example, the saintlike person who has inherited no less than eight parts of the Spirit of Light and only one of Darkness would rejoice in "eyes that are black and glowing," and have a curly beard, subdued speech, and fine and well-ordered teeth. He would be of moderate build, "neither too tall nor too short," with smooth thighs and fine and tapering fingers. (See the present writer's *Dead Sea Scrolls* [Penguin Books], p. 127.)

This document is unfortunately only fragmentary, and we lack information on the particular constellation that would herald the birth of one whose spiritual inheritance would come entirely from the House of Light. He would be the Prince of Light himself, the long-heralded One who was to come, the Messiah or Christ. We need not look far from Bethlehem to find the source of the Magi story of Matthew's Gospel (chap. 2).

It may well be that Saint Paul has his unbecoming physical appearance in mind when he speaks of the continual war within himself as his inherited inclination to evil struggled with his will to do right. "Wretched man that I am! Who will deliver me from this body of death?" he cries in his torment. "For I delight in the law of God, in my inmost self, but I see in my members another law at war with the law of my mind and making me captive to the law of sin which dwells in my members . . . I of myself serve the law of God with my mind, but with my flesh I serve the law of sin" (Rom. 7:22-25). Certainly the Apostle makes constant reference to his unprepossessing appearance.

He quotes the taunt of his opponents: "His letters are weighty and strong, but his bodily presence is weak, and his speech of no account" (2 Cor. 10:10), and an early tradition describes him as "baldheaded, bowlegged, strongly built, a man small in size, with meeting eyebrows, with a rather large nose, full of grace, for at times he looked like a man and at times he had the face of an angel" (*Acta Pauli et Theclae*, para. 3), just the kind of physiognomy we might expect to find in the Essene astrological work under one of the less happily endowed zodiacal categories. However, for the Apostle his faith in the Savior-god, Christ, was sufficient to overcome his inherited deficiencies, physical and spiritual: By allowing the Spirit of God to take over his mind ("Dwell within him"), he would become with his fellow believers a "son of God":

> But you are not in the flesh, you are in the Spirit, if the Spirit of God really dwells in you . . . For all who are led by the Spirit of God are sons of God . . . When we cry "Abba! Father!" it is the Spirit himself bearing witness with our spirit that we are children of God . . . [Rom. 8:9-19]

It seems that this mystical union with the crucified and risen Savior was not without some physical cost to himself. It is unclear whether his speaking of "a man in Christ who fourteen years ago was caught up to the third heaven—whether in the body or out of the body, God knows . . . and he heard things that cannot be told which man may not utter" (2 Cor. 12:2-4) was a modest reference to himself, or whether it really recalls the trance state of a fellow Christian. But he does claim to have had numerous revelations from similar experiences and suffered, perhaps as a result, from a perpetual "thorn in the flesh, a messenger of Satan, to harass me, to keep me from being too elated" (v. 7).

There is no doubt that the dissociative practices of mystics of all times have usually been arduous and have sometimes proved very dangerous. Ever present was the fear that the free-flying spirit would be prevented by one of the guardian angels of the seven spheres through which the seer must pass from returning to its body; more prosaically, that the man would die from the effects of whatever hallucinatory agent he used before he could recover from his trance. There is an old Jewish tradition, dating from the second century, which tells of four mystics who "entered the garden," as the trance state is called, and only one emerged "in peace"; of the others one went mad, another died, and a third took up magic.

The actual procedures by which the Essene and Christian visionaries, or shamans, and their acolytes released their souls for their journey through the seven heavens to the throne of Wisdom, doubtless involved some kind of hallucinatory agent or mind-numbing exercise. To judge from contemporary experience, some will have used drugs or vapors, or subjected themselves to hypnosis, or used purely physical means like overbreathing, monotonous repetition of words or phrases, stamping, whirling in dance, and the like, or simply underwent prolonged fasting, which we are told can induce the same biochemical effect on the brain.

Commonly, mystics liken their experiences to long journeys ("trips") into other, more fanciful worlds, where sensual impressions are intensified, colors are brighter, sounds are magnified, emotions heightened. The Old Testament records instances of prophets and diviners seeking such trance states to receive their divine communications; and, in the case of King Saul, his schizophrenic behavior was difficult to distinguish from the uncontrolled ravings of the professional prophets (1 Sam. 10:9-13; 19:24). The colorful and exotic visions of the prophet Ezekiel were of more lasting influence. From his place of exile in Babylonia, the seer saw in a trance the divine chariot accompanied by strange winged creatures, the Cherubim, supporting a throne bearing God himself, resplendent in glory. From this fiery, flashing vision of the divine presence, the source of heavenly *gnosis*, the prophet received his mission and message to his fellow exiles:

> And above the firmament over their heads there was the likeness of a throne, in appearance like sapphire; and seated above the likeness of a throne was a likeness as it were of a human form. And upward from what had the appearance of his loins I saw as it were gleaming bronze, like the appearance of fire enclosed round about; and downward from what had the appearance of fire, and there was brightness round about him. Like the appearance of the bow that is in the cloud on the day of rain, so was the appearance of the brightness round about. Such was the appearance of the likeness of the glory of the Lord. And when I saw it, I fell upon my face, and I heard the voice of one speaking. And he said to me, "Son of man, stand upon your feet, and I will speak with you." And when he spoke to me, the Spirit entered into me. . . . [Ezek. 1:26-2:2]

On the basis of this biblical reference subsequent Jewish mystics fantasized on the theme of the heavenly chariot and produced a whole body of unrestrained theological speculation that Rabbinic Judaism had some difficulty in countering. This kind of mysticism still flourished in medieval times, but it is clear from the Scrolls that the theme of the divine chariot and the vision of heavenly Wisdom was already the focus of esoteric speculation at the turn of the era:

> The Cherubim praise the vision of the Throne-Chariot above the celestial sphere, and they extol the [radiance] of the fiery

firmament beneath the throne of His glory. And the Holy Angels come and go between the whirling wheels, like a fiery vision of most holy spirits; and around them stream rivulets of molten fire, like incandescent bronze, a radiance of many brilliant colours, of exquisite hues gloriously mingled. The Spirits of the living God move in constant accord with the glory of the Wonderful Chariot. . . .

Chariot imagery continues in the New Testament, where the apocalyptist of St. John's Revelation is granted the vision of the Word of God, conceptualized by word-play as the "Lamb" (Hebrew *'imerah*, "word"; Aramaic *'imera'*, "lamb"). The writer thus ingeniously combines the sacrificial aspect of Christ's earthly role as the Passover lamb, sacrificed for the sins of the people ("Behold the Lamb of God who takes away the sins of the world": John 1:29), with his pre-existent nature as the Creative Principle, the Logos, Word, seated at the right hand of God:

At once I was in the Spirit, and lo, a throne stood in heaven, with one seated on the throne! And he who sat there appeared like jasper and carnelian, and round the throne was a rainbow that looked like an emerald. . . . From the throne issue flashes of lightning, and voices and peals of thunder, and before the throne burn seven torches of fire, which are the seven spirits of God; and before the throne there is as it were a sea of glass, like crystal. And round the throne, on each side of the throne, are four living creatures. . . . And between the throne and the four living creatures and among the elders, I saw a Lamb standing. . . . [Rev. 4:2-5:6]

Knowledge of God and healing were merely two aspects of the same life-force, the Holy Spirit. The Essenes enumerate the fruits of the Spirit of Truth as:

To enlighten the heart of man and to make straight before
him all the ways of righteousness, to make his heart fearful
for the judgements of God; a humble spirit, an even temper,
a freely compassionate nature, an eternal goodness, and
understanding and insight, and a mighty wisdom that believes in all God's works; a confident trust in his many
mercies, and a spirit of knowledge in every ordered work . . .
a humble bearing and a discretion regarding all the hidden
things of Truth and secrets of Knowledge.

The reward to those who display such qualities in their
lives is

healing and abundant peace, length of life and fruitful seed,
with everlasting blessings and eternal joy in immortality, a
crown of glory, and a robe of majesty in eternal light.
[Manual of Discipline, Col. IV]

The Christians, that is, those who were anointed with the
chrism, or unction, believed that they symbolized and effected
their enlightenment through their anointing:

You have been anointed by the Holy One, and you know all
things . . . the anointing which you received from him abides
in you, and you have no need that any one should teach you;
as his anointing teaches you about everything, and is true,
and is no lie, just as it has taught you, abide in him. [1 John
2:20-27]

The Epistle of James suggests that anyone of the Christian
community who was sick should call the elders to anoint him
with oil in the name of Jesus (5:14). The Twelve were sent out
among their fellow men casting out demons and anointing the
sick with oil (Mark 6:13). Healing by unction persisted in the

Church's rites until the twelfth century and is practiced by Christian faith-healers even today, while the anointing of the dying, the so-called extreme unction, has persisted in the Roman Catholic Church to this day.

Herein lies also the idea of embalming corpses with ointments and spices. They were not expected to halt decomposition, as Martha appreciated in the case of her brother Lazarus, who had been dead for four days (John 11:39), although in Egypt additional measures were taken also to preserve even the flesh. The Hebrew story of Jacob's embalming over forty days uses the word "healers" for the practitioners of the craft (Gen. 50:2), and the verbal root for "embalm" conveys also in its various dialects "to come fully to life, mature," as well as "make spicy." The idea seems to have been to impart life and rebirth to the dead person in the underworld, and the reference to "forty days" reflects an ancient tradition that this was the period of gestation in the womb before the foetus could be considered human. So the two Marys come to the grave to anoint the dead Jesus (Mark 16:1; Luke 23:56), as did Nicodemus, bringing myrrh and aloes for the purpose (John 19:39). Mary, Martha's sister, had earlier anointed Jesus' feet with nard, anticipating his death (John 12:3, 7).

The practical connection between anointing, healing, and the mystical search for the Knowledge of God may well have had something to do with the ingredients of the Essene and Christian unction. They would certainly have included the aromatic gums and spices of the traditional Israelite anointing oil— myrrh, aromatic cane, cinnamon, and cassia (Exod. 30:23-25). Under certain enclosed conditions, a mixture of these substances rubbed on the skin could produce the kind of intoxicating belief in self-omniscience referred to in the New Testament. Furthermore, the atmosphere of the oracular chamber would be charged with the reek of sacred incense, consisting of "sweet spices, stacte, onycha, and galbanum, sweet spices with pure frankincense . . ." (Exod. 30:34), giving the kind of overpowering hypnotic effect referred to by the Church father Clement of Alexandria when he writes of the "frenzy of a lying soothsayer," and his oracles as merely the "intoxication produced by the reeking fumes of sacrifice" (Homilies, III, 13).

The interpretation of the "knowledge of God" inspired under such hypnotic circumstances has always posed problems to the shaman's attendants. It was too often uttered only as a meaningless babble of words or sounds. Saint Paul distinguishes between the gift of "speaking with tongues" and "prophesying," that is, between the uncontrolled utterances of the mystic and intelligible words of comfort and instruction for the community in general:

> Make love your aim, and earnestly desire the spiritual gifts, especially that you may prophesy. For one who speaks in a tongue speaks not to men but to God; for no one understands him, but he utters mysteries in the Spirit. On the other hand, he who prophesies speaks to men for their upbuilding and encouragement and consolation. He who speaks in a tongue edifies himself, but he who prophesies edifies the church. He who prophesies is greater than he who speaks in tongues, unless someone interprets, so that the church may be edified. . . . [1 Cor. 14:1-5]

As far as the practice of spiritual healing is concerned, one may suppose that the induction of a hypnotic state in the patient would be reckoned to assist the process. Practically speaking, this might also have something to do with the healer's use of touch (the "laying-on of hands"), and his apparent need to gaze penetratingly into the eyes of the patient, and to command his no less concentrated attention in return. If the suppliant were also influenced to some degree by the inhalation of some mild intoxicating agent such as could be produced by a highly volatile anointing oil, this might have aided the process of psychological control. Furthermore, the surrounding atmosphere of mystery, and a conviction of the presence of demonic powers must have ensured a heightened emotional state in all concerned. If suggestion plays a large part in faith-healing, as many would affirm, then the psychological receptiveness of the patient has to be of great importance, and all such measures as hypnotism and mild intoxication can be expected to have played their part, without necessarily calling into question the validity of the cures obtained. In any case, for both healer and subject, the essential element was the saving power of God, transmitted to a suppliant whose eyes and heart had been made receptive through faith.

Chapter Four

The Millennium

It is natural enough for us to seek rational explanations for the healing miracles recorded in the New Testament and to try to describe in modern terms the psychological phenomena for which the ancient writers use a more traditional terminology. But this is not to cast doubt on the motives or sincerity of the Essene/Christian Physicians. Of course the stories in the New Testament are not necessarily historical, and, as this writer has tried to show in *The Dead Sea Scrolls and the Christian Myth*, they were probably never intended to be taken literally. But it is quite clear from the Scrolls and the whole history of the Christian Church that from the outset religious healing played an important part in the communities and in the fundamental doctrines of the faith. The miracle stories were partly anecdotal portrayals in exaggerated, dramatic form of important features of the religious life and expectation, much as in the case of the Peter cycle, as we have seen, where the episodes reminded members of the Order in an easily memorable way of the duties and responsibilities of the Guardian/Bishop. But, more important, based as many of them were on biblical prophecy, the miracles were intended to bring home to their audiences the fundamental belief that the appearance of the Christ on earth had inaugurated the apocalyptic period of the Last Days, the immediate prelude to the coming of the Kingdom and the ensuing Millennium.

When we enter the more "realistic" world of the Pauline

correspondence, we find the Apostle constantly anticipating the glorious event of Christ's early return, when the dead would arise and "death would be swallowed up in victory" (1 Cor. 15:54). In this quotation from Isaiah (25:8) the writer is echoing the Old Testament conception of a time to come when all would be peace and harmony, where "the wolf shall dwell with the lamb, and the leopard shall lie down with the kid . . . and they shall not hurt or destroy in all my holy mountain; for the earth shall be full of the Knowledge of the Lord, as waters cover the sea" (Isa. 11:6-9). This idealistic vision of a world without suffering included, of course, the concept of the universal availability of healing, physical and spiritual. Even nature's less desirable aspects were to be "healed," when deserts would blossom, and the "poor and needy" would no longer be parched for lack of water, for

> I, the Lord, will answer them,
>> I, the God of Israel, will not forsake them.
> I will open rivers on the bare heights,
>> and fountains in the midst of the valleys;
> I will make the wilderness a pool of water,
>> and the dry land springs of water . . .
> that men may see and know,
>> may consider and understand together,
> that the hand of the Lord has done this,
>> the Holy One of Israel has created it.

[Isa. 41:17-20]

Among such manifestations of God's healing power, bringing life where there was none, was the transformation of the Dead Sea to a lake teeming with fish, where fishermen might fill their nets to bursting. The stream of life-giving water that would bring about this wonderful change would spring from the threshold of the Temple in Jerusalem and flow into the eastern Galilee (meaning simply "region") in the Arabah, the name given to the Jordan Rift Valley. This was the vision recorded by the prophet Ezekiel in far-off Babylonia during the Exile, in the sixth-century B.C.:

> And he said unto me, "This water flows towards eastern Galilee and goes down into the Arabah; and when it enters the stagnant waters of the Sea, the water will become fresh. And wherever the river goes every living creature which swarms will live, and there will be very many fish. . . . Fishermen will stand beside the Sea; from En-gedi to En-eglaim it will be a place for the spreading of nets; its fish will be of very many kinds, like the fish of the Mediterranean. And on the banks, on both sides of the river, there will grow all kinds of trees for food. Their leaves will not wither nor their fruit fail, but they will bear fresh fruit every month, because the water for them flows from the Sanctuary. Their fruit will be for food, and their leaves for healing. . . . [Ezek. 47:8-12]

It is clear that whatever spring the prophet had in mind when he set the northern limit of the new Galilean fishing grounds at "En-eglaim," the Essenes interpreted it as referring to the little freshwater stream called today 'Ain Feshkha, which runs to waste in the Dead Sea a few miles south of the ruins of their monastery. The apocryphal visions of Enoch, which as we have already noted were a favorite source of inspiration to the people of the Scrolls, also refer to the miraculous stream running eastward from the Temple (26:3), changing the desert into a plantation of "aromatic trees, exhaling the fragrance of frankincense and myrrh" (29:1). Furthermore, they would have identified themselves with the "fishermen" spreading their nets so productively upon the "healed" waters of the Sea, and this was taken up by their Teacher in his hymns:

> Thou hast given me a dwelling with many fishers
> who spread a net upon the face of the waters . . .

[Col. V]

> I [thank Thee, O Lord, for] Thou hast lodged me beside
> a fountain of running waters in a waterless land,
> and by a spring in a parched land,
> and by channels that irrigate a garden . . .

[Col. VIII]

The Essene psalmist identifies himself with the "fountain of living waters" in whom his followers might find the secrets of eternal life:

> But Thou, O my God, hast put into my mouth
> as showers of early rain for all [who thirst],
> and a spring of living water . . .
> Suddenly they shall gush forth
> from the secret hiding places . . .

[Col. VIII]

as Jesus promises the Samaritan woman at Jacob's well:

> Every one who drinks of this water will thirst again, but
> whoever drinks of the water that I shall give him will never
> thirst; the water that I shall give him will become in him a
> spring of water welling up to eternal life. [John 4:13-14]

and the New Testament apocalyptist characterizes Ezekiel's

miraculous stream that would run from the threshold of the Temple to sweeten the Dead Sea as "the water of life":

> Then he showed me the river of the water of life, bright as crystal, flowing from the throne of God and of the Lamb through the middle of the street of the city; also on either side of the river, the tree of life, yielding its fruit each month; and the leaves of the tree were for the healing of nations. [Rev. 22:1-2]

This idea of a holy stream as a fount of inspiration, bringing life and healing into the souls of men, must have seemed especially appealing to the Essene ascetics for whom the parched heat of the desert was no mere figure of speech. The desolate landscape of the Dead Sea shores would have made them more than ever aware of the contrasts between their present "House of Exile," as they call it in one of their scrolls, and the luxuriant herbage promised in the apocalyptic images of the wonderful Thousand Years of the messianic age. Ezekiel's vision of abundant trees along the river banks, with "leaves of healing," might well have seemed particularly appropriate to the Physicians, and the concept recurs in the Teacher's hymns:

> [that they may grow] together, a plantation
>   of cypress, pine, and cedar, for Thy glory,
> trees of life beside a fountain of mystery,
> hidden among all the other trees by the water's edge;
>   so that they may put forth a Shoot
>   for an eternal Planting;
> And before that, establish their own roots,
>   extending them to the watercourse,
> that its cutting might be open to the living waters
> and refresh them from the everlasting spring . . .

[Col. VIII]

The Essene psalmist has, of course, drawn his inspiration in part from Isaiah's vision of the regenerated world of the Millennium:

> When the poor and needy seek water,
>> and there is none,
>> and their tongue is parched with thirst,
> I, the Lord, will answer them,
>> I, the God of Israel, will not forsake them.
> I will open rivers on the bare heights,
>> and fountains in the midst of the valleys;
> I will make the wilderness a pool of water,
>> and the dry land springs of water.
> I will put in the wilderness the cedar,
>> the acacia, the myrtle, and the olive;
> I will set in the desert the cypress,
>> the plane and the pine together;
> that men may see and know,
>> may consider and understand together,
> that the hand of the Lord has done this,
>> the Holy One of Israel has created it.

[Isa. 41:17-20]

The "trees" that were to be nourished by the life-giving stream were the Essenes themselves, and indeed this figure of the Elect as trees, planted and watered by God for his glory, has good biblical precedent in Isaiah's gospel of "good tidings to the afflicted":

> to grant to those who mourn in Zion,
>> to give them a garland instead of ashes,
> the oil of gladness instead of mourning,
>> the mantle of praise instead of a faint spirit;
> that they may be called oaks of righteousness,

> the Planting of the Lord,
> that He may be glorified . . .

[Isa. 61:3]

The Essenes by the Dead Sea could make an even closer identification with themselves in the case of one species of tree that would appear in the wilderness, the myrtles. The Aramaic word for "myrtles" (*'asayya'*) is almost exactly similar to the name of the Essenes themselves, *asayya*, "physicians." The curative powers of this aromatic tree and its leaves were well known and widely applied in ancient pharmacy, and the myrtle wreath has an honored place in the rituals of many religions, not least Judaism.

When the New Testament story-tellers came to dramatize the earthly life of their messianic Teacher in terms of the biblical prophecy of the end-time, they "rationalized" the background. Instead of placing the Master and his fishermen followers in the highly improbable setting of the unregenerated and very "Dead" Sea of real life, they transferred the venue to another "Galilee" (or "region") some way to the north, where there really were fish to be found in abundance, and such miracle stories as Simon Peter's wonderful draught of fishes and his call to become a "fisher of men" (Luke 5:4-10) might seem more "realistic" to the listeners and in character with the general down-to-earth tone of the Gospel narratives. But, fact or fiction, the essential teaching was there for those for whom the stories were intended: The Kingdom of God was among them, and the long-awaited Millennium was soon to dawn. The miracles of healing were signs of the times to those who looked eagerly for "him who was to come":

The disciples of John told him of all these things. And John calling to him two of his disciples, sent them to the Lord, saying, "Are you he who is to come or shall we look for another?" In that hour he cured many of their diseases and plagues and evil spirits, and on many that were blind he bestowed sight. And he answered them, "Go and tell John what you have seen and heard: the blind receive their sight, the lame walk, lepers are cleansed, and the deaf hear, the dead are raised up, the poor have good news preached to them. . . . [Luke 7:18-22]

The good news that the Gospels were meant to convey was that God had entered the world and had decreed the end of Satan's rule. From then on the demonic powers that brought men low in sickness and diseases over which they seemed to have no control had met their match. It was a message of hope, and whenever the Physicians brought relief to the suffering of those who came to them in faith—and one cannot doubt that by some means or other, through psychological persuasion or the use of traditional medicaments, real cures were effected at their hands—that hope was confirmed in men's hearts. In a harsh world that seemed to grow ever more cruel, ruled by imperial masters growing increasingly powerful and less concerned for the rights of individuals, the idea that even the humblest of God's creatures might be assured of His love was a profound inspiration, and it has remained so ever since.

Chapter Five

"Physician, Heal Thyself . . ."

The quotation in the title of this book and in our chapter heading is, of course, from the story of Jesus' attempt to preach the gospel in his own home town of Nazareth:

> And all spoke well of him, and wondered at the gracious words which proceeded out of his mouth; and they said, "Is this not Joseph's son?" And he said to them, "Doubtless you will quote to me this proverb, 'Physician, heal thyself: what we have heard you did at Capernaum, do here also in your own country'." And he said, "Truly, I say to you, no prophet is acceptable in his own country." [Luke 4:22-23]

The proverb that seems here to be cited is unremarkable and must have its parallel in any social situation where the "expert" singularly fails to cure his own ills, whether he be a plumber, automobile engineer, marriage guidance counselor, or doctor. We may suspect in the case of the Jesus story that the proverb seemed to have a particular relevance if, as has been suggested, the "Christians" of the religious groups among whom the cycle of stories and sayings circulated were otherwise known as Essenes, "Physicians." Of more immediate interest is the content of the address that the Master gives his unappreciative home-town audience:

> The Spirit of the Lord is upon me,
>   because he has anointed me
> to preach good news to the poor.
>
> He has sent me to proclaim release to the captives
>   and recovering of sight to the blind,
> to set at liberty those who are oppressed,
>   to proclaim the acceptable year of the Lord.

[Luke 4:18-19]

As every Bible student knows, this apparent quotation from the Scriptures appears nowhere in this form in the Old Testament: It is a combination of citations from Isaiah (61:1-2; 58:6) with an allusion to Psalm 146 (vv. 7-8), and includes a reading from the Greek version rather than the Hebrew original, which reads "those who are bound" (as a verbal parallel to "captives") in place of "blind." It is the kind of literary device familiar to us from elsewhere in the New Testament and in Jewish literature generally, including the Dead Sea Scrolls, where a chain of biblical phrases is used to give some particular teaching the air and authority of Scripture, adapting the words of the sacred text to suit the purpose, rather than citing exactly any single passage, word for word. Where we find such instances of a somewhat free—not to say, cavalier—treatment of the biblical text, the reader should look carefully at the changes that have been introduced into the quotation, assuming, as one might, that the scribe and his source were well aware of the exact wording of the original and regarded its integrity with as much reverence and awe as was customary in such religious circles. A careful comparison with the Old Testament passages quoted in our story will show that the overall result of the literary eclecticism has been to emphasize the liberating nature of the proclamation: The Day of the Lord, the appearance of the Messiah, has brought freedom from oppression and, along with it, healing of the afflicted.

We have seen already that the Millennium that the Messiah was to inaugurate by his coming was to be marked by a rejuvenation in nature, involving extraordinary fertility of land and beast, an abandonment of instinctive aggression between species, and a general alleviation of suffering. The Nazarene "Physician" in the Lucan story announces that the power of healing that he has brought with him from God can only be exercised in an environment that is free from prejudice. Where men were blinded by their own preconceptions about the Messiah, he was unable to relieve the afflicted of their spiritual or physical infirmities. Part of the messianic mission, apparently, was to free mankind from such constraints, to open people's mental eyes to spiritual realities and thus pave the way to the totally transformed world of the new order. The same message is conveyed by the story of Jesus' encounter with the "Jews" who "believed in him" (John 8:31-36; the modern reader cannot help but be surprised at the extraordinarily disinterested way in which the, presumably Jewish, evangelists speak of "the Jews" as if they were themselves of some other ethnic group—a reflection of the Greek gentile milieu in which the writings had their currency and for which they were primarily intended):

> Jesus then said to the Jews who had believed in him, "If you continue in my word, you are truly my disciples, and you will know the truth, and the truth will make you free." They answered him, "We are descendants of Abraham, and have never been in bondage to any one. How is it that you say, 'You will be made free?'" Jesus answered them, "Truly, truly, I say to you, every one who commits sin is a slave to sin . . . if the Son makes you free, you will be free indeed. . . ."

Jesus, as Messiah, is here again offering to free the Jews from the spiritual blindness to which their Jewish exclusiveness threatened to condemn them. As "sons of Abraham" they felt no need of freedom; the Master replies that a greater servitude than economic slavery was that imposed by "sin." Saint Paul, in his letter to the Romans, echoes the same theme:

> There is therefore now no condemnation for those who are in Christ Jesus. For the law of the Spirit of life in Christ Jesus has set me free from the law of sin and death. [Rom. 8:1-2]

The term *sin* here is not merely moral turpitude, but an attitude of mind, a spiritual blindness arising from a sense of guilt or fear. For the Essene Christians, faith in their Master, be he the Teacher of Righteousness or Jesus (if they are not, as this writer affirms, one and the same), was the means of attaining the Knowledge of God in their hearts, and thus the confidence to be free. Healing was primarily a matter of releasing the mind of the patient from inhibitions about himself, whether in respect of his standing with God or with his fellows, that restricted his ability to avail himself of the opportunities now offered. The New Age had dawned that offered him a fresh opportunity to be himself, mentally and physically. Healing was essentially a *restoration* of nature to what was intended at the Creation:

> And God saw everything that he had made, and behold, it was very good. [Gen. 1:31]

It was a manifestation of "truth," that is, a realization of God's purpose in nature unmarred by demonic corruption, or, as Saint Paul would say, the "law of sin."

The Essene Manual of Discipline looks to this New Age

when truth would triumph in the hearts of men, and he would by God's grace be able to overcome his spiritual inheritance for good or ill:

> But God, in the mysteries of his understanding and the wisdom of his glory, has appointed an end to perversity and at the time of visitation he will destroy it for ever. Then truth, which up until the day of Judgement has lain befouled in the byways of wickedness during the dominion of perversity, will come forth into the world for evermore. Then God will purify by truth all men's deeds, and will refine for himself man's substance by obliterating all perverse inclinations from his flesh, and cleansing him by his holy spirit of all his wicked deeds. Like purifying waters he will sprinkle upon him the spirit of truth, [washing] him clean of all abominations and falsehood. And he will be immersed in the purifying spirit so that he can instruct the upright in the knowledge of the Most High, and teach the wisdom of the angels to those who walk uprightly. For God has chosen them for an everlasting Covenant, and all the glory of Adam shall be theirs. And there will be no more perversity, and the works of deceit will be put to shame.
>
> Until now the spirits of truth and error have struggled against each other in men's hearts, so that they walk this way and that in wisdom and folly. According to his inheritance of truth, so a man hates folly, and in proportion to his lot from the realm of perversity, so is he wicked and loathes the truth. For God has allotted the two spirits in equal measure until the appointed end, and the Renewal of all things. . . . [Col. IV]

So the New Dawn would bring to mankind a reunification of the human spirit, divided hitherto by the warring factions within man's personality. From then on all creation would be marked by a harmony of purpose unmarred by conflicting aims and desires. The universal peace and understanding that the prophets envisaged would not be imposed from without, but would spring from that inner peace in the heart of every man that was the first fruit of the spirit of truth.

Chapter Six

Religion in Revolt

Religion is man's response to repression; its power is proportionate to the need.

In Palestine, the domination of Rome drove Jewish idealists toward Zealot extremism on the one hand, and the Essene fatalism on the other. The one brought the destruction of the Temple and the Diaspora; the other the eventual transformation of an esoteric and exclusive messianism into a universal cult of a Savior-god, more Greek than Jewish, more humanist than theocratic. Rome's power declined, and in the fourth century the "Great Church" achieved the political power it had been seeking, but over the corpses of its gnostic enemies and amid the smoking ashes of their libraries. Thereafter the history of the Church has seen the recurring resurgence of gnostic individualism, struggling to free itself from the stifling formalism of hierarchical mediation and to exert the believer's right of direct access to his God. While the Church protected the faithful from the rapine of their political masters, its own exactions have been reluctantly accepted; but, where an authoritarian priesthood has itself become corrupt and joined its own oppression to that of the State, the frustrations of individual believers have found outlets in new forms of zealotism that have threatened the unity of Christendom.

In almost all cases these "heresies" have embodied the principles of gnosticism that we have seen already in the Dead Sea Scrolls and in parts of the New Testament, notably the

writings of Saint Paul and those commonly designated Johann-
ine (as seeming to share a common philosophical approach
with the author of the Fourth Gospel). The most readily recognizable of these features have been a dualism of opposing
cosmic forces, symbolized as light and darkness representing
good and evil, and some degree of asceticism, a renouncing of
the material world and an exaltation of things spiritual. The one
thesis leads almost inevitably into the second, since, if the earth
and all creation is evil, then the inborn instinct of man for
seeking godliness must be a fruit of the spirit within him, "at
war with the law of the flesh," as Saint Paul would say. The
dilemma of dualism—whence, then, came evil, if not from
God?—remained unresolved, as of course it must in any theistic
philosophy. If God is good, then he cannot be credited with
evil works, unless, with the Greek tragedians, he is regarded as
cynically outside the pale of normal justice, and man as his
plaything of an idle hour.

   Christianity has tried to resolve the problem by arguing
that man has brought evil upon himself by rebelling against
God's will, but that a loving Creator has throughout history
offered his children successive opportunities for restoration to
primeval bliss in return for repentance and the resumption of a
divinely ordered way of life. But this is unsatisfactory, since the
very concept of free-will assumes the possibility of a choice
between good and evil, leaving the existence of the latter in a
world created by a beneficent deity still unexplained.

   The gnostic "heresies" offered various solutions to the problem that so beset Saint Paul: how to overcome the constant
temptation to act against his better judgment, or win the "war
in his members." At the one extreme they condemned all
material things as the creation not of God but of the devil, to
be utterly rejected and as far as possible ignored in a life of
extreme asceticism and spiritual contemplation; at the other

extreme they argued that since the world was evil, it was of no account, and society's attempts to regulate men's lives were equally worthless. They therefore ignored man-made laws and lived their lives with reckless disregard for the usually accepted norms of social behavior. Such doctrinal extremes, however, were not realizable in practice by any but the selected few; most believers were obliged by sheer necessity to find a compromise. The ascetics eschewed marriage, or any form of sexual gratification; observed strict dietary disciplines; avoided any activity likely to harm other creatures, human, animal, or vegetable; and concentrated their mental energies on the glorification of God and the acquisition of his *gnosis*. Believers of lesser rank were content to serve the "Perfect," as they were sometimes called, and to save them compromising their "purity" by procuring their basic necessities and through their own restricted sexual activities ensuring continuing generations of acolytes.

But the essential feature of gnostic religion, of whatever persuasion, was that the individual was a free spirit, however strict or lax the discipline of his particular order. Some of the rituals by which he achieved his union with the source of Knowledge may seem to us bizarre, if not downright obscene, but through them his mentors sought to lead him into the blessed state of inner illumination by virtue of his own filial relationship with God, not as a suppliant of the priest or through the medium of ecclesiastical or angelic intervention. In the words of the Essene psalmist:

> For Thou wilt bring Thy glorious [salvation]
>   to all the men of Thy council,
> to those who share a common standing
>   with the angels of Thy Presence.
> There shall be no mediator among them [to invoke Thee],

and no messenger to [carry back Thy] response . . .
for they themselves are answered
    from out of Thy glorious mouth;
and they shall be princes
    in the company of [the angels].

[Hymns, Col. VI]

In such an atmosphere of spiritual immediacy, the healing
tradition, which was a continuing feature of Christian life,
depended more on the believer's own faith than upon the
ministrations of the professional physician. His community
leaders may have been the dispensers of herbs, unctions, and
manipulative treatment, and advisers of therapeutic regimens,
like any lay practitioners in the art; but for the humble believer
the greater contribution to his cure must come from within himself. The sun that brought healing in its wings must rise in his
own heart before it could make him whole. The demons had to
be exorcised by the combined forces of the Cephas/Caiaphas
and the patient, the discerning eye and the responsive faith.

Where Church pastors had the trust of their people, this
sense of personal involvement on the part of the individual
believer need not be absent even from an intercessory ministry:
The shepherd led his flock and did not drive them, and they
appeared together before the Throne of Grace. When the
Church through its history has sought to dictate its authority,
suppress individualism, and impose humiliation rather than
preach humility, the ancient genius of the faith has exerted
itself in revolt, and the faithful have exercised their right to
seek their own way to their heavenly Father and realize their
true selves.

The tremendous cultural, social, and economic changes of
the eleventh and twelfth centuries in Europe also witnessed

some of the greatest challenges to the Church's unity. With the increase in trade, which had remained stagnant after the collapse of the Roman empire, population increased, particularly around the towns. More efficient agriculture meant not only that these extra mouths could be fed but that famine elsewhere gave opportunities for the export of food by entrepreneurial merchants who became a significant new class of bourgeoisie between freeman and noble. The Church hierarchy found itself having to come to terms with a rising feudal monarchy throughout Europe, and at the same time to institute its own urgently needed internal reforms. There had been a general decrease in religious fervor and even morality among the clergy; and amid the awakening appreciation of classical literature and values, the standard of literacy of many of the incumbents was too often woefully inadequate to meet the challenge of their better educated parishioners. Their numbers, also, were insufficient to provide the Church's offices for the larger urban populations, and with the loosening of ecclesiastical control the zealous individualism of the Faith, never far beneath the surface, exploded into a number of "heresies" that seriously threatened the Church's authority.

One of the most remarkable of such movements was that of the Cathars (Greek *katharoi*, "pure"). It flourished in western Europe in the twelfth and thirteenth centuries, and its doctrines bore all the marks of its gnostic predecessors: the dualistic division of the universe and its accompanying ascription of all material things to the creation of Satan; and man as an alien and sojourner in an evil world, whose aim must be to free his spirit, which was essentially good, for reunion with its divine Source. The Cathars believed in the ultimate redemption of God's spirits, but only after successive incarnations; the souls of the dead returned to possess the bodies of other men, and even beasts, animals being no less blessed with souls. Despite the rigidity of its regimen for the "Perfect," its celibacy and extreme asceticism—even to the point of approving of suicide—Catharism held an extraordinary attraction for many kinds of people, among them unprivileged lower clergy, poorer knights, merchants and artisans of the new trading class, and well-educated men and women who found the cult a means of self-expression and spiritual fulfillment denied them by an unsympathetic and often inadequate Church.

Furthermore, Catharism proved itself no mere evangelistic crusade, an emotional outburst that burnt itself out in a year or two; it became organized into a church, with its own hierarchy, liturgy, and system of doctrine. Its first bishop established himself in the north of France around 1149, and in a few years there were similar sees founded in southern France and in the Lombardy region of Italy. There is no doubt that this gnostic flame had been brought west by the so-called Bogomils, a similar sect of much earlier eastern origins, but which flourished in the Balkans between the tenth and the fifteenth centuries. Their dualistic philosophy and ascetic disciplines brought them into conflict with the eastern arm of Christendom, the Orthodox Church, and they denied the Incarnation of Christ, rejected baptism and the Eucharist, refused to believe in miracles, spurned the cross, indeed the whole impedimenta of ecclesiastical regalia and buildings, and the priesthood in general. Even their fiercest opponents had to acknowledge the austerity of their lives, and they have been called "the greatest puritans of the Middle Ages." And yet this religion that required of its followers to live without marriage, wine, eating meat, and just about everything that for most people makes life pleasant or even bearable, became accepted not only by the poorer classes of society but in Bosnia by the rulers and nobility, and later developed into a national movement. In Bulgaria itself Bogomilism remained a powerful force until the fourteenth century, and it was not until the Ottoman conquest of eastern Europe that the movement subsided. So powerful was this gnostic revival in its heyday, and the spread of its influence, that by the thirteenth century, the movement had formed a single network, stretching from the Black Sea to the Atlantic.

It seems on the face of it a strange contradiction that a religious doctrine that denies the flesh and applauds asceticism should at the same time have given impetus to the practice of faith-healing. If the body is evil, why seek cures for its ills? The Gnostics' answer would have been that the emphasis for them was not on maintaining the health of the body but on the cure of the soul: If the spirit was right with God then the mind and body would maintain a balance that would resist the power of evil. If one sought simply a remedy for ague, warts, or any other common ailment, then by all means consult the local wise man or woman, the midwife, or the pedlar in herbal remedies; pay your money and take your chance. But the religious Physician was primarily a doctor of the soul, whose success was not measured in terms of a lowered temperature or safely delivered baby, but in terms of a quiet mind, an assurance of sins forgiven, and a sense of self-confidence and spiritual integrity.

The Church, Orthodox and Catholic, took a terrible re-venge against the rebels. The crisis that confronted the estab-lishment was reckoned as threatening to its existence, as that first division when the gnostic sects refused to deny their individualism and ally themselves with the so-called Great Church for the sake of political protection and the promise of self-aggrandisement. The reaction of the Church's leaders was comparable: to burn out the "heresies," destroy their literature, and make examples of those who had dared to challenge the true Faith. At the center of the Byzantine empire, in Constanti-nople itself, the Bogomil leader Basil was publicly burnt about

1100; and his followers, many of them aristocrats, were tried and imprisoned. In 1184 papal and secular power combined to issue a decree laying down the procedure for ecclesiastical trial, following which the accused heretic was handed over to the secular arm for punishment. This could mean confiscation of property, exile, or even death, but already tradition had established burning at the stake as the most suitable punishment for the unrepentant heretic. The terrible Inquisition was beginning to cast its shadow across the religious face of Europe.

Pope Innocent III (1198-1216) is said to have believed that conversion to orthodoxy was preferable to the use of force; but in the face of obdurate Cathars who thought their right to worship God was at least as well established as the Pope's, and whose piety and sobriety offered no excuse for persecution, contrasting as it did with the dissolute lives of many of the clergy, the pontiff was forced to the conclusion that systematic extermination was a more effective means of removing heresy than persuasion. Although the Cathars' main support came originally from the artisan class—from which they were commonly known as the Weavers—in Provence particularly they won the hearts of the nobility, most notable of whom was Raymond VI, count of Toulouse. He resisted demands to recant, and when, on January 15, 1208, the papal legate was himself murdered, the Pope found the excuse he needed to call a religious crusade to rout out the evil—not this time against the pagan Muslims who dared to claim their holy shrines in Palestine as their own, but against a Christian noble who had supported heresy in his own domains. A group of barons from northern France seized their opportunity to pay off old scores and supplement their income with loot from Raymond's treasuries, and rode forth to ravage Toulouse and to massacre the inhabitants. Almost inevitably the victims included Catholics as well as Cathars, there being little opportunity in the heat of battle to enquire too closely into the precise nature of their religious beliefs. Those that were not cut down with the sword, they hanged, and exhibited their bodies on Raymond's battlements, a warning to all of the need to conform. It is said that by the end of the crusade, the whole region of Septimania, between the Rhone and the Pyrenees, had been reduced to a desert. In 1244 the fortress of Montségur, near the Pyrenees, where a large commune of the Perfect had made their home, was captured and destroyed along with its pious inhabitants. The Cathars who remained went underground, while some fled to Italy where persecution was less violent or sustained.

The Church had learnt its lesson. Gnosticism was not dead; constant vigilance was needed to ensure that such dangerous schisms within Christianity were not in future to be allowed to take root and develop unchecked. Early in the thirteenth century the Dominican order of learned preachers was founded to tour the country provinces and counter heresies whenever and wherever they might show themselves. Not unnaturally they were also the best people to spy out the enemies on the ground, and to offer evidence before the newly established ecclesiastical courts of inquiry, the infamous Inquisition. When religious freedom again raised its head in Europe, the flame was not so easily extinguished, and in the Reformation much larger territories, and millions more hearts, were lost forever to the Great Church.

Chapter Seven

Religion Reformed

The Reformation was born out of spiritual frustration. Its leaders elevated revelation above mediation, the biblical Word above the sacraments. In the course of time their followers too often substituted the tyranny of bigoted sectarianism for papal politics and subjected their people to agonizing dilemmas of conduct and belief through doctrinaire interpretations of Scripture; but those early enthusiasts were intoxicated with the scent of freedom and entranced with the vision of a return to a simple faith and an unregimented community of believers. They had no need for priestly intercession, for each man and woman knew God as Father, and their spirits responded with His spirit, recognizing the identity of their Source and their substance. Thus the healing functions of the new faith took on an intimacy and immediacy they had not known since the days of the gnostic Physicians. The arbitrary favor of the saints, sought too often through the purses of avaricious mendicants peddling their relics and holy water, could be bypassed. Believers who had been chosen and justified by faith alone could claim their right to importune God directly, as children their father. Those who now came forward as faith-healers were not necessarily clerics but simple men who believed themselves to be channels of grace through whom the Spirit of healing might work directly upon the suppliant.

Luther's emphasis upon "justification by faith," which was the keynote of his theology and that of later reformers like

John Wesley, meant that believers no longer sought salvation by their own efforts, or through the medium of the Church's sacraments; they could rest content in the knowledge that, if they were among God's elect, divine grace was theirs for the asking. They had only to believe that Christ had died for them and they could be assured of their restoration to divine favor. Since God was essentially a God of love, yearning for the return of souls to their predestined state of grace, the suppliant would be met more than halfway in his quest for salvation. In terms of faith-healing, this meant that the believer brought to the practitioner an open, relaxed mind, which has always been the essential first step to any form of therapy. To his question, "What can I do to be made well again?" echoing the anguished pleas of the jailor to Paul and Silas, "Sirs, what must I do to be saved?" (Acts 16:30), the answer was, simply, "There is nothing you can do except believe that God loves you and wants you to be restored to the state of mind and body to which He called you, and which is the only condition He recognizes." In the words of Saint Paul's exhortation to the Romans:

> I appeal to you therefore, brethren, by the mercies of God, to present your bodies as a living sacrifice, holy and acceptable to God, which is your spiritual worship. Do not be conformed to this world but be transformed by the renewal of your mind, that you may prove what is the will of God, what is good and acceptable and perfect. [12:1-2]

That kind of humanitarian response, offering hope and assurance to the sinner and the sufferer, was in marked contrast to the attitude to be expected of an authoritarian Church still struggling with the unresolved problem of the origin and purpose of evil in a morally directed world: that sickness was a divine chastisement intended as a warning or punishment to the sinner, or as a means by which the saint could exercise even greater virtue in passive acceptance of affliction. In the words of a nineteenth-century Catholic theologian, P. Lejeune:

> Illness is the most excellent of corporeal mortifications, the mortification which one has not one's self chosen, which is imposed directly by God, and is the direct expression of his will. [*Introd. à la Vie Mystique*, 1899, p. 218]

Or, again, as expressed by another Catholic divine:

> If other mortifications are of silver, this one is of gold; since although it comes of ourselves, coming as it does of original sin, still on its greater side, as coming (like all that happens) from the providence of God, it is of divine manufacture. And how just are its blows! And how efficacious it is! . . . I do not hesitate to say that patience in a long illness is mortification's very masterpiece, and consequently the triumph of mortified souls. [Both quotations from William James, *The Varieties of Religious Experience*, 1902, p. 113, n.1]

It has to be remembered that the religious Reformation of the sixteenth century was not an isolated phenomenon: It was part of a much wider broadening of spiritual and intellectual horizons. Furthermore, the ideas then put forward so dramatically by Luther and his contemporaries were not new; the spirit of freedom had been abroad for some time, as we have noted, and some of the old gnostic movements, like that of the Waldenses, born and nurtured in remote Alpine valleys from at least the thirteenth century, and the anti-clericalism of their spiritual cousins the Hussites, had maintained a living witness to individualism in worship and opposition to the established Church through centuries of violent persecution. Among the earliest congratulatory delegations received by Martin Luther were two members of the "Bohemian Brethren," as the Hussites were called, welcoming him to the struggle they and their friends had been waging long before he nailed his ninety-five theses to the door of the Wittenberg church.

The Reformation succeeded because it came at a time when a newly awakened nationalism in Europe was flexing its muscles, and it was convenient for those rulers concerned to find a religious cause to assist them in their resistance to Rome's domination. The unity of Church and State, once the safeguard of western civilization, was a hindrance to nationalist ambitions, and so the movement for spiritual independence found a political support it had hitherto lacked. It was also a time of intellectual rediscovery. The reawakening of interest in the classical writers of pagan Greece and Rome, which was the hallmark of the European Renaissance, stimulated a revival of learning in the ancient languages of Greek, Latin, and Hebrew, and an appreciation of textual integrity. These studies gave scholars the tools for making those vernacular translations of the Bible that the new emphasis on the Word of God necessitated.

In the field of scientific medicine men began to feel free at last to go beyond and even repudiate the venerated traditions of such ancient writers as Hippocrates, Galen, and the medieval Persian "prince of physicians," Avicenna. To much that had been soundly observed and shrewdly assessed by these scholars, the Church had added Christianized versions of popular astrological superstitions, like the replacement of the signs of the zodiac, to which parts of the human body were referred, with various patron saints: St. Blaisius for the throat and lungs, St. Apollonia for the teeth, St. Erasmus for the abdomen, St. Lucia and St. Triduana for the eyes, and so on. Other saints were considered to provide protection from, or cure of, diseases reckoned to be their particular province, such as St. Vitus for chorea, or St. Vitus's dance, and St. Anthony for erysipelas, or St. Anthony's fire. In particular need of reform were traditional conceptions of human anatomy and physiology, studies of which had for so long been hindered by superstitious or religious reservations about dissecting the body, and the sixteenth century saw an upsurge of unrestricted research in Europe, correcting many of Galen's errors and viewing the human body not as dead anatomy but as a living and active organism. Not all went the lengths of the strangely compulsive Paracelsus, who is said to have prefaced his lectures at Basel by publicly burning the works of Avicenna and Galen, but there was in general a willingness to explore new fields and to experiment, perhaps even dangerously, with new techniques.

With increasing scientific research into the origins of disease and a more realistic understanding of human anatomy, religious healing was free to pursue its own course as a supplement to more "practical" medicine. If today religious healers are treated with more respect, even by scientific bodies careful to preserve a strictly rationalist stance, it is because their contribution can be assessed on its own merits, without the awe and veneration demanded by an all-powerful Church claiming that through its ministrations alone can a supplicant seek the healing power of the Knowledge of God.

William James, at the beginning of this century, expressed the "liberal" concept of religion and scientific medicine in this way:

> The experiences which we have been studying . . . plainly show the universe to be a more many-sided affair than any sect, even the scientific sect, allows for. What, in the end, are all our verifications but experiences that agree with more or less isolated systems of ideas (conceptual systems) that our minds have framed? But why in the name of common sense need we assume that only one such system of ideas can be true? The obvious outcome of our total experience is that the

world can be handled according to many systems of ideas, and is so handled by different men, and will each time give some characteristic kind of profit, for which he cares, to the handler, while at the same time some other kind of profit has to be omitted or postponed. Science gives to all of us telegraphy, electric lighting, and diagnosis, and succeeds in preventing and curing a certain amount of disease. Religion in the shape of mind-cure gives to some of us serenity, moral poise, and happiness, and prevents certain forms of disease as well as science does, or even better in a certain class of persons. Evidently, then, the science and the religion are both of them genuine keys for unlocking the world's treasure-house to him who can use either of them practically. Just as evidently neither is exhaustive or exclusive of the other's simultaneous use. And why, after all, may not the world be so complex as to consist of many interpenetrating spheres of reality, which we can thus approach in alternation by using different conceptions and assuming different attitudes . . . On this view religion and science, each verified in its own way from hour to hour and from life to life, would be co-eternal. Primitive thought, with its belief in individualized personal forces, seems at any rate as far as ever from being driven by science from the field today. Numbers of educated people still find it the directest experimental channel by which to carry on their intercourse with reality. [*Varieties of Religious Experience*, pp. 122-23]

Many of us would question the validity of this well-meant attempt to equate religion and science in terms of objective reality, not least since the former philosophy does not allow of the kind of experimental verification demanded by a scientific discipline. Nevertheless, the results that can be achieved in terms of relieving human suffering by recourse to religious persuasion are often comparable to those obtained by more "scientific" means. Whether in either case the results can in the long run be justified by the means is a matter for individual assessment, but there are dangers in the manipulation of the mind quite as real, and possibly more insidious, than those associated with the use of drugs or surgery.

Chapter Eight

Religion Rejected

The old prophetic vision of a world restored to some pristine state of innocence and inexhaustible productivity, like all such myths of the Golden Age, past and to come, is a necessary fantasy, a resistance to despair, an assertion of man's will to survive. An animal faces each threat that confronts it with its allotment of instinctive reactions—recognition, challenge, or flight—without the need for reasoned consideration. Man crossed the threshold of Homo sapiens by evolving a mind and an imagination. Thereafter he bore with him not only the most powerful of all weapons against other animals and natural hazards but also a major handicap—recognition of the odds stacked up against him. While aware of his own physical inadequacy, he had yet to believe that the battle to survive was worth fighting, that somewhere across the hill or over the horizon there was some better land, an Eden where nature was more bountiful, dangers no longer threatened, and pleasure could be had without pain. He peopled that imaginary paradise with fallible mortals like himself but surrounded them with an environment and a set of deities whose only purpose was to serve mankind, to offer warmth, food, and surroundings conducive to exercising those pleasures that made life worth living.

> Then God said, "Let us make man in our own image, after our likeness; and let him have dominion over the fish of the sea, and over the birds of the air, and over the cattle, and over all the earth, and over every creeping thing that creeps

upon the earth." So God created man in his own image, in the image of God he created him; male and female he created them. And God blessed them, and God said to them, "Be fruitful and multiply, and fill the earth and subdue it; and have dominion over the fish of the sea and over the birds of the air and over every living thing that moves upon the earth." And God said, "Behold, I have given you every plant yielding seed which is upon the face of all the earth, and every tree with seed in its fruit; you shall have them for food. And to every beast of the earth, and to every bird of the air, and to everything that creeps on the earth, everything that has the breath of life, I have given every green plant for food." And it was so. [Gen. 1:26-30]

It has proved the most longlived, and possibly the most disastrous, myth in man's repertoire of egocentric self-delusions. It has enabled him to survive Ice Ages, extreme Arctic cold, and desert heat, famine, plagues, and the predations of his own kind, but it has given him also an exaggerated idea of his own place in the natural order out of all proportion to the fortuitous circumstances of his evolution and his continuing dependence on his environment.

There was not, is not, and never will be a Garden of Eden. The best that man can ever achieve in an evolutionary order based on the survival of the fittest is the maintenance of a kind of ecological harmony with the world about him, with his fellows, and with himself. Where he has come to terms with his limitations, and has acknowledged that greed is followed by dearth, and that the domestication of land and animals carries a responsibility of good husbandry, he has succeeded tolerably well. Where he has taken without replacing, destroyed without repairing, offended without remorse and recompense, he has perished.

The humanist refuses to believe that he is other than evolution has made him—a remarkable, and probably ill-fated, deviant of the ape family whose overdeveloped brain has given him abilities and ideas above his station. To some extent, and for a certain time, he can control his own environment, and even his further evolutionary development, but it is with the realization that the more specialized he makes his lifestyle and genetic conditioning, the more insecure is his viability in a hostile world. Homo erectus, "thinking" man's predecessor, moved across vast areas of the planet, through many varied ecological conditions, because he was capable of adapting to changed circumstances by drawing upon the inherited resources of a rich gene-pool. Such were the many strands in his mammalian stock that the most extreme conditions could be met by the restoration of some dormant feature of his evolutionary past, or the selection of a random mutation that might meet the contingency. Selective breeding after he attained the status of a tribal Homo sapiens, when factors other than physical strength and agility, fleetness of foot, manual dexterity, and the like, were allowed to enter into his choice of a breeding partner, weakened that stock, reduced the gene-pool, and made him increasingly dependent for survival upon a stable ecological and social environment. So vivid became his imagination, so paralyzing his fears, that he dared no longer venture beyond his immediate territory or away from his tribe without inventing a protective, all-seeing deity to hear his prayers. Even death, that most gentle analgesic, assumed in anguished contemplation the uncertainty of a lonely immortality. Fear bred aggression, alienation, and more arrogant assertiveness. He became jealous even of the gods he had created, and tried to emulate them, "to become as one of us, knowing good and evil," demanding more dominance over his fellow creatures and unhindered exploitation of even more natural resources.

Modern technology promises the power to control and to

harmonize the natural world, and for many people has superseded the concept of a Creator-god, continually balancing the seasons, dearth and plenty, illness and good health. Yet today there is more interest evinced in faith-healing than ever before, even in nonreligious circles. Partly this has to do with a greater awareness in medical quarters of the close relationship between mind and body; the term *psychosomatic* has taken its place in even the layman's vocabulary. He knows that psychological stress can result in hormonal imbalance and physical disorders and is daily warned in the media of the dangers of overanxiety and the blessing of regular relaxation. But there is also a parallel renewal of interest in the ecology, of the dangers of overexploitation of the natural world, and of man's pollution of the planet and its atmosphere. Never has there been such grateful appreciation by the town-dweller of the beauties of the countryside, nor has he sought so avidly for the isolation of deserts and wastelands that have hitherto known only the wandering nomad and religious recluse.

Similarly, the rationalist is aware that the Gnostics' yearning for inner peace, the union of the human spirit with the divine source of grace and knowledge, is realizable in nonreligious terms. He may express that conviction in as many varied ways as there are theologies, and try to achieve it by mental and physical exercises no less demanding than those imposed by the old ascetic orders, but essentially he wants to free his mind from the guilts and anxieties that beset him, to know and come to terms with his own nature, and so give his body the chance of curing its own disorders. This is no less faith-healing than the religionist who seeks from God the forgiveness of sin as the necessary preliminary to restoring his sight or taking up his bed and walking.

The nonbeliever feels no call to be perplexed by the existence of evil in a world created by a beneficent deity. He knows that the nature of the evolutionary process must produce periodic disharmony, but also that it restores the balance in a rhythmic cycle of deprivation and reparation, as the tides ebb and flow, and the sap rises and falls. Man achieves inner peace when he can synchronize his mental and spiritual energies with nature's pulse, and when by the quality and consistency of his life he can avoid the disruption of that harmony by actions and attitudes that Saint Paul would have described as the response by the "unspiritual man" to the "law of sin" within him.

The freedom of thought and religious constraint that was sought and eventually achieved by the medieval Gnostics and their successors of the Reformation has its parallel today in the call by modern man for his liberation from the demands, no less stultifying and emasculating, of an overzealous bureaucracy. The so-called Great Church sacrificed its religious heritage on the altar of uniformity. Its leaders dreamed of a community of the faithful with one canon of Scripture, one creed, one hierarchy, one Pope ruling one empire, sustained with the aid of one army under one discipline, the vision of the perfect ecclesiastical machine. The dream never came true, but not for want of trying. It failed because the faith it inherited called not for a mindless obedience to the demands of a tribal deity and his war lords but for the willing response of individual believers to a God of love. The Gnostic Christians and their Essene predecessors may have differed among themselves and at various times on the nature of the world and the manner of its creation, but all believed that there stood at the heart of the universe a harmonizing Spirit with which the humblest suppliant could communicate and to which in time his own soul might be united.

The modern welfare state has something in common with the authoritarian Church. It, too, believes that it can drive its people to the throne of grace by dispensing meal-tickets like indulgences, and ushering its sinners into the "confessionals" of professional counselors, psychiatrists, doctors, and remedial clinics, while holding in reserve the last means of persuasion to conformity, its inquisitional courts and censors' bonfires. The free-thinking rationalist needs room to breathe, to experiment, to seek his own salvation in his own time. The heretical Gnostics were as aware as their orthodox opponents of the advantages of political conformity and compromise, of the security of an ordered life, safety from alien hostility, and a ready access to the saints of healing and their priestly dispensers of charms and herbals, but they elected to stand outside the system. They had to find their own way to God, and the healing they sought began in their hearts and minds.

Suddenly, it seems, we have paused to draw breath. Undoubtedly the threat of nuclear devastation, uncontrolled population growth, and the frightening magnitude of our technological advance over the past few decades has had some part in the recent more modest re-evaluation of man's place in the universe and our more realistic assessment of the finite nature of those resources upon which we must still depend for survival. Not since the onset of the first agricultural revolution some nine or ten thousand years ago has man had so seriously to take count of the laws of ecological balance in weighing his dues against his responsibilities. He has been forced to think of himself as a gifted animal among other living beings, a part of creation, not its lord. That realization, long overdue, has brought down his horizon from imaginary paradises in the heavens, or Edens nestling between ever-flowing streams of plenty, to the immediate world about him, the delicacy of its balance and viability, and the wonder of its powers of renewal despite all man's depredations. And now, amid all the excitements of a computer age when mankind is attacking new frontiers of knowledge and physical endurance, he has paused to learn again the secret of life, of inner harmony and the confidence to compromise. He wants to know when to resist, and when to relax, when to speak out, and when to listen, and above all he desperately wants to know himself, and to recognize his strengths and his limitations. It was this inner tranquility the Gnostics sought when they prayed for the Knowledge of God in their hearts, to become one with the harmonizing Spirit of the universe, and that is where they started in their quest for the healing of their minds and bodies: "Physician, heal thyself . . . ."

Subject Index

Abba, Father, 33
abdomen, 12, 68
Abraham, 16, 51, 52
acacia, 46
acolytes, 34, 57
Acta Pauli et Theclae, 33
Acts, Book of, 22, 23, 24, 25, 26
Adam, 53
administration, 19, 23
aggression, 51, 75
agricultural revolution, 59, 78
agriculture, 59
ague, 61
'Ain Feshkha, 43
Akkadian, 21
alienation, 75
Aloes, 38
Alps, 67
anachronisms, 17
Anah, 12
analgesic, 75
Ananias, 25
anatony, human, 69
anecdotes, 23, 41
angels, 30, 33, 36, 53, 57f.; fallen, 10, 11, 14, 16, 18; guardian, 25f., 34
anoint, 37, 50
Anointed One, *see* Messiah
Anthony, Saint, 68
anti-clericalism, 67

antidotes, 16
antinomianism, 57
anxiety, 76
ape, 75
apocalypse, apocalyptic (*see also* John, Saint), 45
apologists, Christian, 17
Apollonia, Saint, 68
appreciation, of nature, 76
aptitude, spiritual, 78f.
Arabah, 43
Arabic, language, 21
Aramaic, language, 20, 21, 47
Arctic, 74
Ark, 10
army, ecclesiastical, 77
aromatic cane, 38; gums, 38; tree, 47
artisans, 60, 62
'asayya', "myrtles," 47
'asayya', "physicians" (*see also* Essenes), 7, 47
asceticism, 8, 32, 45, 56, 57, 60, 61, 76
ashes, 46
Asphaltitis, Lake, 12
assertiveness, 75
assurance, 66
asthma, 12
astrology, 9, 21, 31, 33, 68
Atlantic, 61

81